PUNCH DRUNK MOUSTACHE

VISUAL DEVELOPMENT FOR ANIMATION AND BEYOND

FOREWORD BY ALICE A. CARTER

designstudio|PRESS

Copy Editor: Laura Huffman
Book Design & Production Layout: Wilfred Castillo
Photography Credits: John-Paul Balmet,
Will Nichols, Quincy Stamper, Nate Watson

Published by Design Studio Press
8577 Higuera Street
Culver City, CA 90232
http://www.designstudiopress.com
E-mail: Info@designstudiopress.com

1098765432

Printed in China
First Edition, July 2013

Library Of Congress Control Number:
2013935809

ISBN-13: 978-193349280-3

CONTENTS

Foreword by Alice A. Carter   page 6
Introduction   page 7

FROM CHICKENS TO WAR
Amy Beth Christenson   page 8

INSATIABLE DESIRES
Max Lim (Hyunwoo Lim)   page 22

CREATURE HUNTER
Jeff Sangalli   page 36

DRIFTING
John-Paul Balmet   page 50

MO-SU-TE-SU
Will Nichols   page 64

XB3
Nate Watson   page 78

PHYLO'S RITE OF PASSAGE
Sean Pando   page 92

RAIN MAKER
Chris Voy   page 106

About the Artists   page 120
Acknowledgments   page 122
Afterword by Colin Fix   page 124

FOREWORD

Punch Drunk Moustache: Visual Development for Animation and Beyond features artwork and stories from a group of eight entertainment industry illustrators. The book not only demonstrates the skill each brings to their profession, but also showcases work developed outside the constraints of studio deadlines and budgets. Every story is as unique as the artist who created it. Together, they demonstrate that imagination unfettered can create a world where the unexpected is commonplace and where humor coexists comfortably with sophisticated imagery.

Although visual-development art came of age in the late twentieth century, the tradition that inspired it began in the 1860s. During the Civil War, American publishers realized that illustrated periodicals outsold the competition. The result was illustration's "Golden Age," a period between the 1860s and the 1930s when American magazines provided an international showcase for artists. Beneficiaries included the great realist Winslow Homer, political cartoonist Thomas Nast, illustrator and muralist Edwin Austin Abbey, and author and illustrator Howard Pyle, who not only created more than 3500 illustrations, but was also an esteemed teacher.

Pyle's instruction produced artists like N.C. Wyeth whose body of work included illustrations for classic children's literature. Pyle student Jessie Willcox Smith became famous for her illustrations of children and painted every cover of *Good Housekeeping* magazine from 1917 through 1933. Following the First World War, illustrator Frank Schoonover commemorated the American forces in a series of paintings published in the *Ladies' Home Journal*. The critical and financial success of Pyle's students inspired legions of other illustrators who in their turn produced iconic images. Among the best known are J.C. Leyendecker and Norman Rockwell.

In the latter part of the 20th century, photography increasingly replaced artwork in books and magazines. Although the long tradition of excellence had produced extraordinary artists, the market for their work declined. What rescued many careers was an inventive patron who understood that regardless of the venue, illustrators had the imagination and skill to bring stories to life. Filmmaker George Lucas once thought of becoming an illustrator himself, so it is not surprising that he would emerge as a key figure in revitalizing the profession. In the early 1970s, when he was struggling to realize his vision for *Star Wars*, Lucas asked illustrator Ralph McQuarrie to produce a series of drawings and production paintings for the film. The artwork McQuarrie created helped to convince executives at 20th Century Fox to fund the project.

Over the years, other artists followed McQuarrie to Lucasfilm for the chance to create images for the growing franchise. Their successes yielded opportunities that now provide careers for visual development artists worldwide. The artists represented in *Punch Drunk Moustache: Visual development for Animation and Beyond* are worthy heirs to this legacy. Their debt to the past is evident in their masterful artistic skill, which is a credit to their profession and its distinguished history. Their connection to the often irreverent and always unpredictable present shines in flashes of wit that enliven ingenious tales of fantasy and wonder.

—Alice A. Carter

INTRODUCTION

Punch Drunk Moustache is a weird name. It might make you giggle, scratch your head, or smile, just like the artists and artwork the name represents. It's a little wild, a little crazy, and a whole lot of fun. We are an eclectic group—a band of misfits. Eight separate artists with eight separate approaches, unified by our love of stories and the visions those stories inspire.

The *Punch Drunk* crew is comprised of working concept designers, illustrators, and comic artists. We all have day jobs that involve imagining for a living. All of us have experience in the field of animation, especially visual development. Animation is a place where anything can happen, as long as one can dream it.

The challenge and the thrill of building a visual world drives us, but we require a starting point. Sometimes a simple word or a side comment can spiral out of control, and soon a whole new project evolves out of thin air.

So it was with *Punch Drunk Moustache*. We thought of a dream project; something unique to each of us that we were violently passionate about, a project we simply had to do. This book is the result.

We hope you have as much fun reading it as we had making it!

FROM CHICKENS TO VICTORY

Amy Beth Christenson

I read more than I draw. I especially love reading early science-fiction authors, and Herbert George Wells is among my favorite storytellers. For this series of images, I started with his novella *The Food of The Gods and How It Came to Earth*. Mankind engineering its own destruction is a common theme for most authors, but the visuals of bringing it about through giants was a refreshing and inspiring take for me. It was a very entertaining read and instantly conjured up some vivid images in my mind. The H.G. Wells story was published in 1904. The giants were created mostly out of scientific curiosity, and there was no wartime element in his original story. The notion of mankind weaponizing a growth formula, however, and using it as a military strategy seemed like a logical progression of the original idea. Hence, I re-imagined the story as it might have happened during World War I. I also reckoned on the fact that fighting giants would be more entertaining than giants that are just sitting around. And for a little more spice, I added in a nod to other H.G. Wells-inspired technology, such as giant air fortresses, reverse-engineered German tripods, and space zeppelins. For the kids out there.

Scientists successfully test super-growth serum, Code name: CRONUS

Governments seize CRONUS, conduct first tests on humans

Colossi presented to public for first time

Tensions rise, countries race to make advances & set up defenses

Invasions begin, a Great War is declared

Major cities begin to fall

Battles escalate with advancement of technology

Entire countries are rendered uninhabitable by humans

Population forced to board airships to survive

Dying planet is left to the Colossi

There is a mass exodus

For humankind to find a new home

INSATIABLE DESIRES

Max Lim (Hyunwoo Lim)

I like history. I enjoy seeing documentary films and also reading books related to history. My hobby is researching photos and videos that are historically related. They are great inspiration, which helps my creativity. I will speak on the subject of three elements, which have been historically contested by humans.

Life

I was inspired by the great king of the East named Qin Shi Huang. He had completed a large empire, and after building his empire, he wanted to live forever. He ordered his army to find the secret of immortality.

He died before he found the answer. Even though he did not find what he wanted, he still left a huge cultural influence after he passed away.

Water

I think water is one of the most important sources of life. All living things need water. Scientists are now searching the universe for the source of water, because they know this will enable them to solve the mystery of life outside of Earth. So I chose finding water as a central source of my main story line.

God

Many believe that God is eternal. This separates us from God. Humans have been searching for immortality, not just to live forever, but to be like God.

Eternal forest The forest holds the water of eternal life. The wise man found the forest's secret here.

On the way to the ancient city, this place had a famous clear sky and green grassland, but it began to dry out.
This is the entrance pass through the ancient city in fog.
The weather became too dry, so many people stopped going to the place.
There are many tiny tribes and animals here.

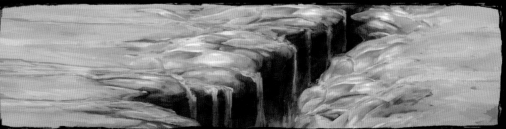

The grassland is drying up.

The grown rock is more than 5000 years old.
Rock worship is found in many cultures of the world.
Many grown rocks spurt out the fog of life while they grow.

NIMA (explorer)
She is the Half-Blood mixture of human and mermaid.
She can breathe freely in the water.

HISTORIA (the wise man)
He uses all tribal languages and an ancient language.
He researches the secret of eternal life using his vast knowledge.

This huge building is one of the towns.
One hundred to five hundred people live in one town.
They work by fishing or hunting.
The fog stones always make mist that surrounds the towns,
so residents turn their lights on every day.

Rocks are getting bigger at the village.
The rocks always provide fog and water because they fume incessantly.
The village was not caught by the Queen, so it is the last of its kind.

The city is far away from the fish tribes.
Tribal deportees arrived here before the last city lost water and energy.

KAL NAL

Queen of the fish tribes.
She was a benevolent person by nature.
She believes in eternal life and steals
the energy and water of the outside world
for immortality and her tribe.

SALA SIN

New right-hand man of the Queen.
He approached the Queen because he has
a grudge against his accursed father.

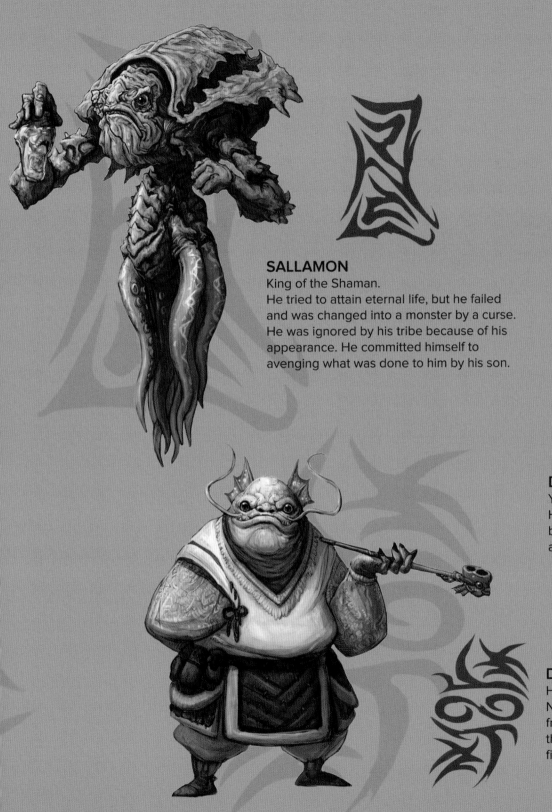

SALLAMON

King of the Shaman.
He tried to attain eternal life, but he failed and was changed into a monster by a curse. He was ignored by his tribe because of his appearance. He committed himself to avenging what was done to him by his son.

DU RI

Younger brother of toad.
He is a cold-hearted and quiet person, but he lends his help to the explorer and the wise man.

DU KO

He was a loyal subject.
Now he is unjustly accused and expelled from the finny tribes. He is helping the explorer and the wise man for his finny tribes and Queen.

The Goddess of Water
She is said to know the secret of immortality.

The Water Goddess and the Ancient City
A long time ago, ancient humans desired eternal life like
the gods. Unfortunately, the gods chose to destroy them.
The goddess lives alone and controls the water.

All water begins on the way to the ancient city.

CREATURE HUNTER

Jeff Sangalli

San Francisco is full of extraordinary, exotic, and weird creatures that are hidden from the average person's gaze. They live in unexpected places... underneath a tea garden bridge, in the dusty old vacuum cleaner, in the hidden places in the park, and at the bottom of the wishing well. They lurk in the basement in the warmth of the furnace in her aunt's old pink house. *Creature Hunter* seeks these mysterious beasts out. She rides the hilly, foggy, windy roads of the city on her motorized bicycle, camera slung over her shoulder, ready to capture them on film.

Sometimes they live in her imagination, like in far-off lands she's seen in books or the pungent foods that her great aunt cooks. They come in all types, shapes and sizes, some pointy and some lanky, some kind and some cranky. She doesn't mind their different moods as long as they don't think she's food. She chronicles her adventures on her bedroom wall, and will have stories to tell when school starts next Fall.

Jim Henson has been a big inspiration for me throughout my life. I grew up watching *The Muppets* and *Sesame Street* and I can still remember the first time I saw *The Dark Crystal*. The realization that someone could bring their imagination to life, inspired me to draw and create.

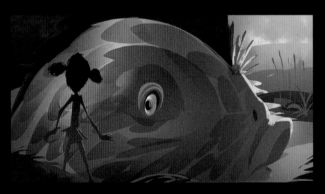  

DRIFTING

John-Paul Balmet

Visual Development

Obviously there is a visual component (it's in the name!), but what exactly is developed? Characters, environments, mood paintings, and props are the most common components, but where does the core inspiration come from? In the earliest pre-production phase, inspiration can come from something as nebulous as a phrase or a word; sometimes it can come from a question. Sometimes inspiration comes from a script or a design brief. Wherever the inspiration comes from, the concept designer needs to have a target to aim at. If there is no target, the designer must make one.

My favorite way to work is from a script. A story creates a thrilling series of limitations on the artist. The artist has to hit the marks the story establishes, yet remain open to pushing against those boundaries to see how far they will stretch before breaking. With a tight script, a character must carry themselves a certain way, dress a certain way.

They will be shaped a certain way. When I can find that life visually, those are my happiest design moments.

This story is an amalgamation of years of false starts and dead ends that somehow evolved into *Drifting*. Author and teacher Brian McDonald said in his indispensable book *Invisible Ink*, "...remember always to tell the truth, the whole truth, and nothing but the truth. If you do this always, you will be a master storyteller. This is much harder than it sounds." I am relatively new to writing, but maybe I was able to tell at least a *little* truth with this project. There is still so much to learn, but as my characters find, the journey is the adventure!

Mother and her two children waited in the yard of their small house on the edge of the gas fields. Grandpa arrived in his dusty old van, jutting his head out the window with a grin.

"You two kids ready for adventure?" he called to Rilo and BB. "Hop in, time's-a-wasting!"

BB held her mother's hands and waited for permission to leave. She was very excited. It was her first trip away from home for more than one day.

"Go ahead BB," Mother laughed. "Just make sure you take care of your brother...Grandpa too." BB leaped into the van and took her seat next to Grandpa. She smiled up at him and he gave her a mischievous wink.

"Come on Rilo," Grandpa called. "Helios frog migrations only happen once every 120 years. We don't want to miss it!"

"You don't want to miss it. I'd rather stay home." Rilo kicked at the dirt-crusted tires on the back of the van. The tip of his new shoe was covered in dust. He frowned.

"Rilo, your father and I want you to get out of the house for once. It will be good for you. Now don't be rude, and I will see you soon," Mother said sternly.

"Fine," Rilo said with an exasperated sigh. He took his seat in the back of the van.

"And heeeeere we go!" Grandpa roared. The van sailed down the road towards the open land beyond the refineries and chemical air.

BB was full of questions: Where do the helios frogs live? How many will we see? What is their home like? Can I hold one? Are they friendly? Are they cute?

"Ha! You don't want me to spoil the surprise do you? You will see for yourself tomorrow," Grandpa said.

"Aw. I want to know! What makes them float? Are they like balloons filled with helium? Do they croak with squeaky voices?"

"Hmm, I wonder what that would sound like?" He gave BB a sly sideways glance.

"Burrripp!" BB chirped in a high-pitched squeak. She giggled.

"Wait, let me try. BURRIPP!" Grandpa's attempt was so silly that he and BB erupted in laughter. Rilo was not amused. He took out one of his ear-bud headphones.

"You guys are so annoying. Is it going to be like this the whole time?"

"Come on Rilo. We're having fun. You shouldn't be afraid to be ridiculous sometimes. I admire BB's curiosity. At least she doesn't have her head buried in a video game."

"Gimme a break. She's just a suck-up."

"Hey, I'm not a suck-up! I just want to know stuff. It's better than being a sad sack in the back. 'Ooh I'm Rilo, I'm so cool. I don't like anything!'" BB made a grim face that was her best impression of her brother. She stuck out her tongue.

"Come on you two. Let's try to get along. We still have a ways to go and there's no point in fighting. It's wild country where we are heading. We have to stick together." Grandpa glanced at Rilo in the rear view mirror expecting a response.

"Wild country?" Rilo scoffed. "It just looks like a bunch of boring nature junk."

"There are a lot of things to watch out for. There are tick bats and bubblers... but first we have to watch out for bergens. They come out at night and are attracted to light.

We'll make our camp up high so the bergens will not be able to reach the tent."

"They're really big! I saw them in my science book!" BB exclaimed.

"Bergens. Uh huh," Rilo said half listening. He continued to play his game and ignored the rest of the conversation.

The van eventually pulled up to a rock formation near the edge of a dense forest.

"Here we are," said Grandpa. "Let's get our stuff up to the top of that little plateau before it gets dark. Rilo, put the game away. BB, I'm going up the rope ladder, then we can set up. Let's get some rest tonight. It's a big day tomorrow!"

Grandpa fixed a light dinner of soup, bread, and some berries with sugar for dessert. They drank hot tea to keep them warm before going to sleep for the night.

"Tomorrow, we will head out down the fire road towards the migration site. We should wake up early so we can get a good viewing spot. Many people have waited their whole lives to see the frogs, so it may be packed. All right you two, sleep well."

Grandpa got into his sleeping bag and quickly began to snore. BB fell asleep soon after. Rilo was not tired. He turned his game on and began to play. The light from the game filled the tent and woke BB.

"Rilo, I'm trying to sleep!" she groaned.

Rilo turned his game off and waited for his sister to fall asleep again. Grandpa's snoring grew louder until it sounded like a sighing jackhammer. Rilo stared up at the roof of the tent as he lay on top of his sleeping bag; bored and unable to sleep.

He slowly and carefully unzipped the tent so as not to wake Grandpa or BB. He sneaked out of the tent, unrolled the rope ladder, and climbed down. Rilo waved his hands, groping in the darkness until he found the van. He opened the side door, climbed in, and turned his game on.

"Bergens. Gimme a break," he scoffed.

Rilo played his game happily until he felt a sudden creeping paranoia wash over him. The hairs on his neck stood on end. He turned around and was terrified to find a giant creature staring into the back of the van window. The creature pushed against the glass repeatedly until it began to crack. Rilo panicked. He looked at the glowing game in his hand and dropped it. He burst out of the the van door and desperately fumbled on hands and knees trying to find the ladder to safety. He finally grasped a rung and climbed as fast as he could. He quickly yanked the ladder up. The screech of metal echoed into the night as the bergen tore the van to pieces.

"Rilo!" Grandpa shouted. He burst out of the tent with his headlamp shining to find Rilo standing on the edge of the plateau. His grandson was dirty and bruised, but seemed intact. Grandpa shined his light down towards the clearing and saw a bergen looking up at him from the wreckage of the van. He grabbed Rilo and headed back into the tent.

Grandpa knelt down and inspected his grandson. Rilo was in shock.

"Are you okay?"

"I didn't mean to," Rilo whimpered. Grandpa embraced him in a bear-hug.

"You gave me a scare Rilo! A big scare. You can't go running off in the night. I told you this is wild country. You don't know anything about it so you need to listen to what I say if you want to stay safe. Now what did you do?"

"It was an accident," Rilo was still distant. His eyes were glazed over.

"We'll talk about it in the morning," Grandpa said. "Right now, you go to bed."

BB stared at Rilo as they lay in their sleeping bags. He turned away. Eventually they all fell asleep until morning arrived.

"WAKE UP!" Grandpa shouted. It was light out and Rilo was still in his sleeping bag. He got up and out of the tent. Grandpa and BB were down below sifting through the wreckage. Rilo climbed down the ladder and looked around. The van was destroyed, and all their gear was spread around the clearing.

Grandpa sat in a chair that had been ripped out of the van by the bergen.

"I know what you did, Rilo," Grandpa said. "I can't believe you would disobey me like that. Did you think I was making things up? You're very lucky you're not dead!"

"I couldn't sleep, it was too noisy."

"Too noisy? Too noisy! So you risk your life, wreck the van and now we have to walk down the fire road and hope someone comes by to pick us up? I can't even find the sat phone. I'm sure it was destroyed with everything else." Grandpa sank back into the broken chair. He did not speak for a long while.

Grandpa eventually emerged from his silence. He rose to his feet and let out a weary sigh.

"Okay you two, grab your backpacks if you can find them. We're heading out!"

BB and Rilo gathered their gear and helped Grandpa pack the tent. They walked for hours together. The dirt fire road cut a dusty line into the heart of the dense forest. Rilo lagged behind, distracted by thoughts of the bergen. He looked into the inky blackness of the woods and shivered. What other monstrosities might reside there?

"Rilo, come on!" said Grandpa. "Keep pace if we want to make it out of here by evening."

Rilo was lost in his dark thoughts.

"Rilo!" Grandpa shouted. He walked back to Rilo who stared blankly into the woods.

"Huh?" Rilo was shocked to see Grandpa approach him with fury in his eyes.

"Hey! What did I say? I said you have to keep pace! You have to listen up and pay attention! This is what got us into this mess in the first place." Grandpa was turning red.

"Sorry, Grandpa! Jeez, I'm just walking!" Rilo was embarrassed and frustrated.

"Sorry for this, sorry for that. Sorry doesn't bring back the van, Rilo! You gotta pull your weight son!" Grandpa pointed an accusing finger in Rilo's face.

"I never wanted to come on this trip! Mom made me come out here to who-knows-where with you guys to see some stupid frogs fly! I don't belong out here. Don't you know that? Look what happened!"

Rilo and Grandpa went at each other, arguing, yelling, and blaming. BB turned away in boredom from their shouting match. She played at the edge of the forest until she noticed movement in the underbrush. It was a little pup! He trotted over and licked her hands. BB laughed and petted him. He playfully jumped back into the bushes, just out of reach.

"Hey, where are you going?" she walked after the pup as it moved deeper into the trees. Rilo noticed BB disappear into the forest out of the corner of his eye.

"Stop BB!" Rilo shouted. He ran to the bushes where BB vanished. Grandpa followed. They pushed into the emerald blackness of the forest and called out to her.

BB followed the pup through the trees until she came upon a clearing. The pup stopped in the middle of what looked like the junkyard of a mad scientist. There was a shack and strange decrepit machinery everywhere. Pipes sputtered noxious steam and hot fluids, and the air smelled like sulfur and alcohol.

The pup made a little yelp noise that was returned with a deep growl somewhere in the junkyard. BB was startled by the threatening sound. The pup gave another little bark, and its mother leapt out, snarling and gnashing its teeth. It pounced at BB, but stopped short when a heavy chain attached to the beast's collar held it at bay.

The beast continued to pull at its chain, straining to get at BB. She could only take a few small steps backwards; she was nearly paralyzed with fear. She slowly backed into the forest when she suddenly felt hands grab her and cover her mouth. She was about to yell, but looked and saw that it was Rilo and Grandpa there to save her!

"Shhhh!" Rilo whispered. Together they hid behind some bushes.

A strange man-creature wearing overalls emerged from the shack holding a gun.

"What got into you! You just causing a ruckus agin?" The creature in overalls yelled at the barking mongrel on its chain. He squinted his small eyes and scanned the yard.

BB, Rilo and Grandpa crept away from the junkyard as quietly as possible. They could hear the gun-toting man behind them yelling.

"Shaddap you mutt! Ain't nothin' out here! Spooked by a tick bat, I reckon. Don't bother me agin 'less it somethin' I need know 'bout."

The door to the shack slammed shut. The mongrel-beast let out a few plaintive barks that tapered off in resignation. BB whispered to Grandpa.

"What was that place?"

"Bubblers, BB. I'm so glad we were able to get to you before it was too late."

"What's a Bubbler, Grandpa?" Rilo was visibly distressed. "They don't sound dangerous, but that guy had a gun!"

"I never thought we would have to deal with them, so I never told you. Bubblers are outlaws that live deep in the forests near the sap springs. The sap wells of the trees mix with the natural mineral springs and create a sort of solution that can be distilled into an illegal drink. The Bubblers bottle the solution and sell it on the black market.

"They are paranoid because they are not allowed in the forests. If they are caught, their stills are smashed up and they are thrown in jail. Their methods hurt the trees

and poison the water, so park rangers are always on the lookout for Bubbler camps." Grandpa was sweating. He wiped his brow and looked at his granddaughter.

"Why did you run off, BB? If Rilo hadn't noticed you, it might have ended badly."

BB ran to Rilo and embraced him. Rilo squirmed.

"Thank you, brother! You act like you don't care, but you do! I'm sorry I ran away. That little pup was so cute, I didn't know!" BB held him tightly.

Rilo gave in. He returned the hug.

"No more craziness, okay?" Rilo said.

"Okay," BB replied.

"I think that goes for all of us," Grandpa said. He pulled out a compass, studied the needle, and pointed. "We still have a long way to go until we get out of this mess. Are you two ready?"

Rilo and BB nodded. The three of them walked together quietly through the forest.

They eventually emerged back on the fire road; the grandchildren cheered at the sight of it. Grandpa allowed himself a little grin as he watched them run down the path whooping and hollering in celebration of their escape.

The road seemed endless. They walked and walked until all of them were exhausted. BB dragged her feet and Rilo hung his head. No one complained, but as the shadows grew longer, their spirits sank.

"I don't believe it!" Grandpa suddenly exclaimed. He roused BB and Rilo from their dazed fatigue. "Look up there!" He pointed off into the distance towards something floating in the sky.

"What is it, Grandpa? Oh, are those the Helios frogs?" asked BB.

"I think we are going to be okay, kids. Just a little further now, and we may just be in for a pleasant surprise."

They hurried down the road with renewed vigor. The forest began to open onto a beautiful vista of mountains dotted with rivers and springs. All eyes were on the sky. The air was dense with a million luminous balloons drifting into the atmosphere.

"This is it," Grandpa laughed.

"Oh, Grandpa! It's beautiful!" BB said. "There are so many of them, I could never count them all!"

"There are millions of them, BB. A true sight to behold. No one has seen a migration like this since your great great great grandfather was alive. I can't believe I'm here myself!"

Grandpa patted Rilo on the back. "Well son, we made it. What do you think of all this?"

Rilo looked up at the countless floating frogs. He watched the frogs inflate the membranes on their backs and rise into the atmosphere like balloons.

"Where are they going?" Rilo asked.

"Well, when they rise high enough, they deflate and glide away. Some can travel up to 100 miles from here. Most of these frogs will not make it, unfortunately. Predators or injuries will take them. But for those that do make it, they have a family. In another 120 years their children will rise like this and find new lands for themselves."

"Well," Rilo said, "I'm not the biggest nature guy, but this is pretty cool, I guess." He shrugged. BB gave him a suspicious glance.

"Come on Rilo. This is awesome!" She punched him in the arm.

"You are such a nerd." He laughed and shot BB a goofy look. They both laughed and watched the helios frogs migrate until the sun set. The fading golden light illuminated the membranes of the frogs like glowing lanterns. When the last of the frogs were visible, Grandpa took his grandchildren and looked for someone among the onlookers that could help them get a ride to the nearest town. Some friendly nature enthusiasts were happy to oblige them.

During the ride to town, Grandpa told the harrowing tale of their time in the wilderness to the naturalists. They were riveted. Hearing the tale, Rilo realized that it really had been an adventure he would never forget. He also could not forget that he was responsible for much of the chaos they were thrust into. He dreaded returning home, yet he yearned for the comfort of his own bed.

They drove up the long lonely dirt path to the small house on the hill where Rilo and BB's mother stood guard at the front door. She appeared as a dark silhouette on a rectangle of orange light. Rilo gulped. BB jumped out and ran to her mother.

"Well, I guess this is it. I think I'll be grounded for about a million years." Rilo gathered his pack.

"Probably. But when you get out, I think I know another event that might coincide nicely with your release." Grandpa rubbed his beard, lost in thought.

Rilo turned with a smile and walked up to the house. Grandpa waved goodbye to his grandchildren and his daughter and drove off towards the horizon, into the night.

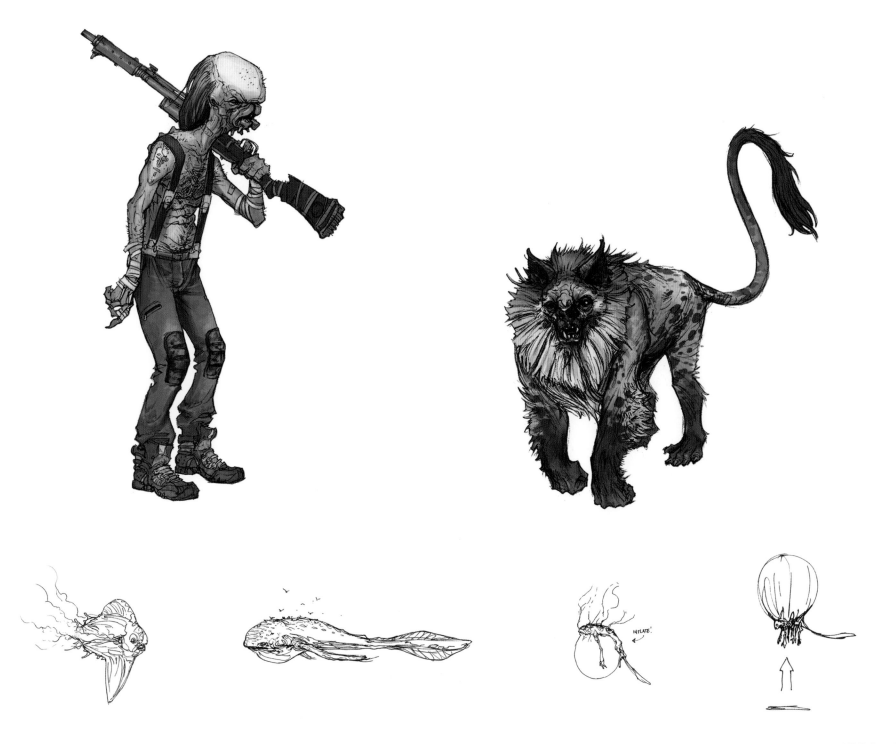

MO-SU-TE-SU

Will Nichols

After many millennia, a little robot comes back from the distant reaches of space to share what he has learned and gained with his creators. Unfortunately those that created him are long gone. In fact, homo sapiens has been classified extinct for quite some time. But he's not giving up! Out there in the cosmos, there must be some humans still left. With bizarre alien races, greedy cyborgs, and attractive bio machines, our hero will jump from one adventure to another searching for his creators and running from those that wish to use his great power for their own nefarious purposes.

In this episode, our hero is on a mission to rescue his biomechanical companion who is in the clutches of a hot and deadly bounty hunter. He, a master of disguise, will penetrate the seedy underworld of alien scum to rescue his trusty sidekick. Will he succeed!? Take a look and see for yourself in this episode of...

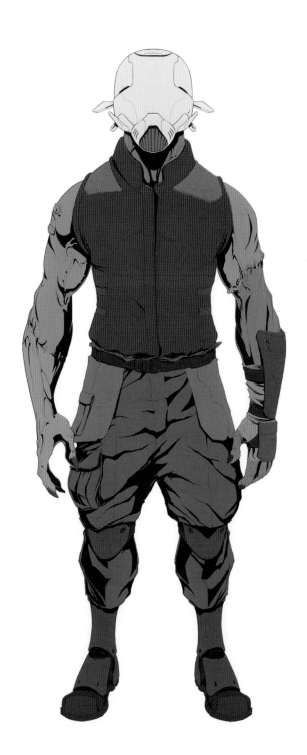

XB3

Nate Watson

In the early seventies, George Lucas had an idea for a space adventure in the vein of the serialized science-fiction stories he enjoyed as a child. It was big, it was risky, and it was awesome. But it was a hard sell. It wasn't until Ralph McQuarrie came aboard Lucas's *Star Wars* project, and put brush to canvas, that the powers-that-be finally realized the amazing mythology that was being pitched to them.

In the early nineties, The Wachowski Brothers pitched their idea for *The Matrix* using what was essentially a comic book adaptation of their first script. With this art, created by the incomparable Steve Scroce, the brothers were able to provide a roadmap outlining their plans for a very ambitious trilogy of films. Again, just like with *Star Wars* twenty years earlier, the executives were able to see the film long before cameras ever rolled.

It's these stories and others like them that inspired XB3. In creating it, I imagined myself trying to pitch the idea of a multimillion-dollar film to execs that wouldn't get it if I'd only described it in writing. XB3 is a fairly simple story featuring a woman running from giant monsters. Part *Jurassic Park*, part *Godzilla*, with a large helping of *Gulliver's Travels*. It's a concept better described in words and pictures. It moves kind of fast in its journey from start to finish—I imagined myself with a precious twenty- or thirty-minute window of very busy people's time.

As you read it, put yourselves in the role of the Hollywood dealmaker. Would you option XB3? And if you did, would you cast Milla Jovovich in the lead role and Rhona Mitra in the role of the warden, like I did in my head as I drew it? I had a blast working on this small story, and while imagining it as a movie pitch was a neat flight of fancy, what XB3 really is, is fun for fun's sake. I hope when you're done reading it, you'll agree. Especially if you happen to be a Hollywood dealmaker.

IN THE SIXTH GRADE, I HAD A P.E COACH NAMED *MR. NICHOLS.* HE WORE THOSE NASTY COACH SHORTS, PULLED HIS SOCKS UP TO HIS KNEECAPS AND SMELLED LIKE OLD SPICE AND *BASKETBALLS.*

EVERYONE HATED MR. NICHOLS, BECAUSE HE LIKED TO MAKE US RUN. A *LOT.* MY BEST FRIEND WOULD FAKE SICK BEFORE EVERY CLASS. HE'D *STILL* MAKE HER RUN.

I DIDN'T MIND. I LOVED TO *RUN.*

I DON'T LOVE IT ANYMORE.

FOUR YEARS AGO, SOME BORED RICH KID OPENED A *DIMENSIONAL DOORWAY* USING AN IPHONE, TWINE AND A VIDEO HE SAW ON YOUTUBE. THE DOORWAY LED TO A WORLD OF GIANT *CREATURES* WHO DECIDED TO COME THROUGH AND MAKE A MESS OF OLD MOMMA EARTH. THE WORLD GOVERNMENTS GOT TOGETHER AND DEVELOPED A PLAN TO GET RID OF OUR OVERGROWN AND UNWANTED GUESTS.

CALLED THE *XB3* PROGRAM, THE PLAN TURNED LUCKY RUN ENTHUSIASTS LIKE ME INTO *BAIT* FOR THE MONSTERS. XB3 IS A MILITARY TERM FOR THINGS THAT ARE EXPENDABLE.

THEY SAY THE TERM WAS NEVER MEANT TO REFER TO PEOPLE. I'M NOT SO SURE.

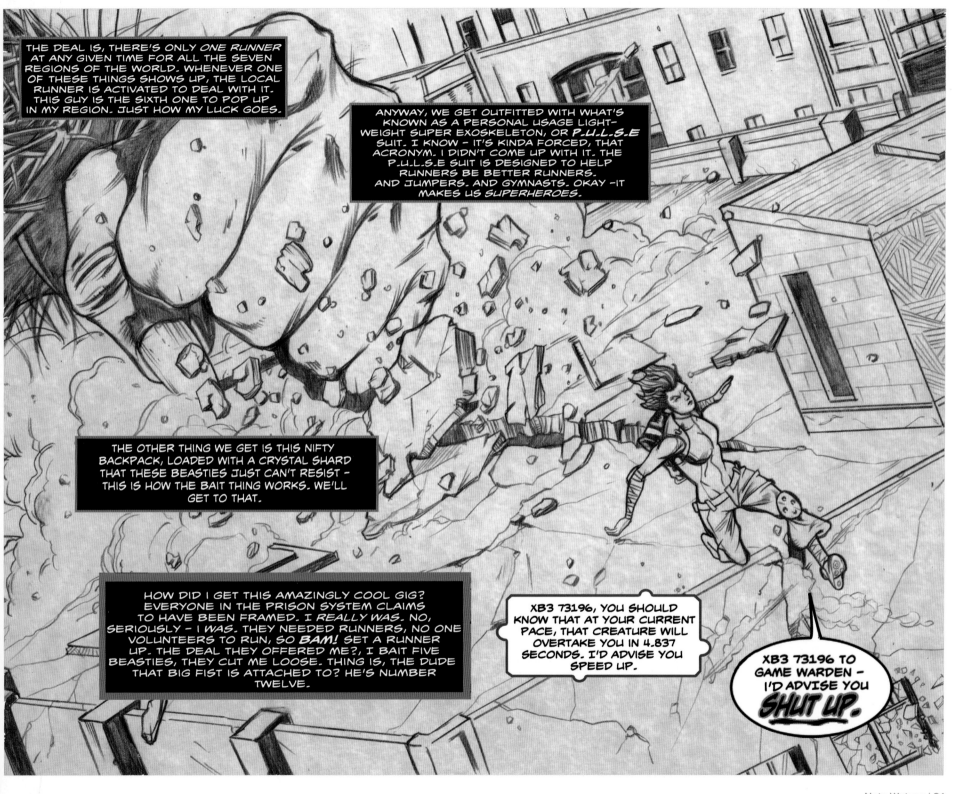

WARDEN MILLA CORBIN.

TWO THINGS WORTH NOTING ABOUT THIS WOMAN – ONE: SHE'S *EVIL* AS HELL AND TWO: **SHE'S EVIL AS HELL.** YUP – SAID THAT TWICE. THAT PART'S IMPORTANT.

I *ASSURE* YOU, ONCE THE ORGANISM IS OFF-EARTH AND YOUR SECONDARY OBLIGATION *FULFILLED*, YOU ARE A FREE WOMAN. WELL . . . FREE AS A WOMAN SUCH AS YOURSELF CAN BE.

WHICH MEANS *WHAT*, EXACTLY?

YOU'RE A *RESTLESS SOUL.* WE'VE DELAYED YOUR PARDON SEVEN TIMES, AND UNLIKE YOUR PEERS, YOU HAVE DONE NOTHING MORE THAN MILDLY *WHINE* ABOUT IT. WHY IS THAT? COULD IT BE THAT WITHOUT RUNNING YOU'D BE LOST?

MAYBE YOU KNOW, JUST AS I DO, THAT THIS WORK GIVES YOU *PURPOSE*. FREED FROM IT, YOU'D QUICKLY BECOME A *PRISONER* OF YOUR-SELF. THIS WORK IS THE ONLY THING YOU HAVE.

IZZAT RIGHT?

UNFORTUNATELY, IT IS – AND I ABSOLUTELY *HATE* HER FOR KNOWING THAT. BEFORE I GOT LOCKED UP, I WAS KINDA THE PICTURE OF A LIFE WELL WASTED – LOTS OF ENERGY WITHOUT FOCUS. I FOUND FOCUS HERE.

THIS IS *THE CHRYSALIS*. THIS IS THE REASON WHY THEY CHASE THE RUNNERS. TOLD YOU WE'D GET TO IT.

NOW I'M NOT SURE *HOW* WE KNOW WHAT WE KNOW ABOUT THIS THING. I'VE ASKED, AND BEEN TOLD NOT TO DO THAT AGAIN. SO I HAVEN'T.

APPARENTLY THESE THINGS COME FROM A WORLD GOVERNED BY A *MONARCHY*. EACH KING SITS ON THE THRONE FOR EXACTLY ONE-THOUSAND YEARS. KINDA LIKE THE QUEEN OF ENGLAND. KIDDING.

ON THE LAST DAY OF THE THOUSANTH YEAR, THE SITTING KING GIVES UP HIS LIFE ESSENCE, RELEASING IT INTO A CRYSTALINE GESTATION CHAMBER. AT SOME POINT (THIS PART WE'RE UNCLEAR ON) THE NEW KING IS BORN.

DURING THIS TIME, THERE IS NO KING. NATURALLY, THERE ARE THOSE WHO FEEL THOUSANDS OF YEARS UNDER THE SAME FAMILY'S AUTHORITY IS KINDA NOT COOL, AND THEY PLOT TO CHANGE THAT.

WHEN THE PORTAL WAS OPENED UP TO OUR WORLD, THEY HIT ON A PLOT THAT ACTUALLY WORKED. THEY *STOLE THE CHRYSALIS* –

– AND *THREW* IT INTO OUR WORLD. DISCONNECTED FROM HIS HOME-WORLD THE NEW KING WOULD *NEVER* HATCH.

THE BAD GUYS WERE SURE THEY HAD WON, BUT THEY HADN'T CONSIDERED THAT THE KING'S SUBJECTS *LIKED* BEING UNDER HIS RULE.

AND UNBEKNOWNST TO THE THRONE STEALERS, THOSE LOYAL TO THE TRUE KING SET OUT TO *RECOVER* THEIR LOST MONARCH.

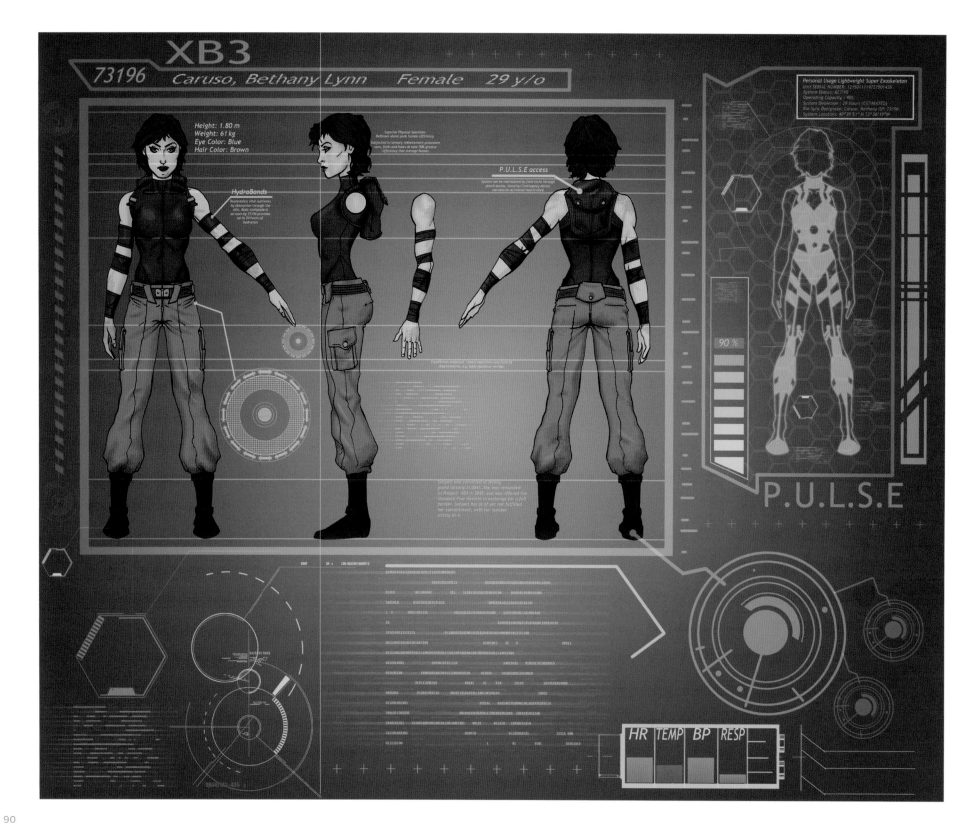

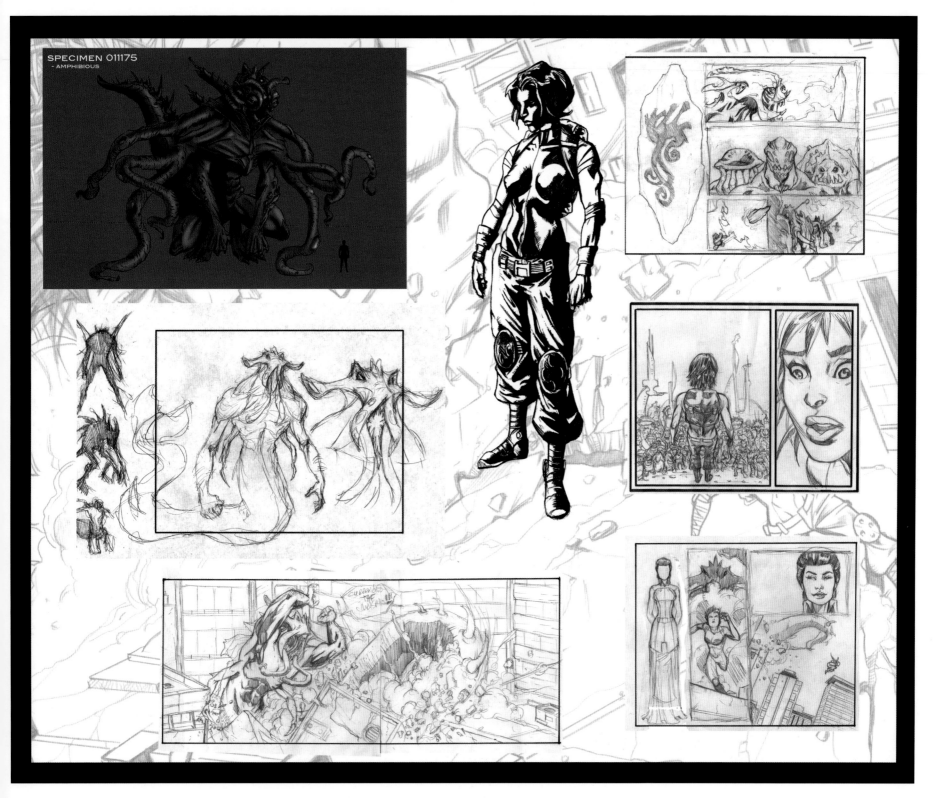

SPECIMEN 01175
- AMPHIBIOUS

PHYLO'S RITE OF PASSAGE

Sean Pando

It all started from a simple sketch. I drew a dart frog with a spear; they seemed to go together. Dart frogs in nature already have such beautiful patterning that resembles tribal tattoos. This and the fact that they are poisonous, inspired a lot of ideas I wanted to try and push further. Plus, it seemed like a great excuse to paint bright colors and rainforest scenes.

The more I studied about poison dart frogs the more ideas I got from interesting facts, like how they aren't born poisonous, but get the toxins from their diet. This, combined with the fact that frogs go through such visible changes as they mature, led me to base the story pitch around a rite of passage. What do they have to do to prove themselves worthy to have this almost magical power of poison skin? What would it look like if it *was* magical? What type of predator would want to stop froglets from becoming poisonous frogs? What if the main character was a runt that still had a tail and was the last one to go on this journey? I tried to answer a few of these questions and to design a little bit of the world that would exist for these tribal dart frogs.

DART FROGS ARENT BORN WITH THEIR STRIPES
THEY MUST BE EARNED

PHYLO

THEIR VILLAGE IS HIGH
UP IN THE TREES

THEY BUILD THEIR HUTS AROUND BROMELIAD POOLS TO RAISE THEIR TADPOLES.

THE TADPOLES SOON MOVE TO BIGGER POOLS AND TRANSFORM INTO FROGLETS

SHAMAN

THE SHAMAN TRAINS THE FROGLETS HOW TO FIGHT.

MOTMOT

PHYLO MUST COMPLETE AN ANCIENT RITE OF PASSAGE TO BECOME A WARRIOR.

HE MUST FACE THE MOTMOT AND BRING BACK A MYSTIC ORCHID.

THE SHAMAN USES THE ORCHID PETALS TO CREATE A MAGIC POTION.

PHYLO DRINKS THE BITTER POTION AND IS TRANSFORMED INTO A POISONOUS FROG

RAIN MAKER

Chris Voy

You may think that the occurrence of rain and the water cycle consists of a series of phenomena in which water molecules change states in accordance with their surroundings: Evaporation, occurring when temperatures become warm enough for water molecules to escape into the atmosphere; condensation, when the air is damp enough for molecules to form into a cloud; and finally, precipitation, once the cloud has become too dense to stay aloft in gas form it turns to water and falls as rain. This rain then replenishes the watershed, flowing to rivers, lakes, and seas. In time, this ancient process begins anew.

This might be what you think, but it is a common misunderstanding.

Actually small faucet people manufacture weather in secret mountaintop factories stationed worldwide. They whistle happy tunes as they deliver rain, sleet, and snow via their flying cloud machines. Occasionally, territorial disputes arise between competing seasons resulting in violent clashes of thunder and lightning. The losers of these battles fall to the earth below where they are captured and taken to hidden watersheds and are worshipped by the thirsty umbrella people of the rainforest.

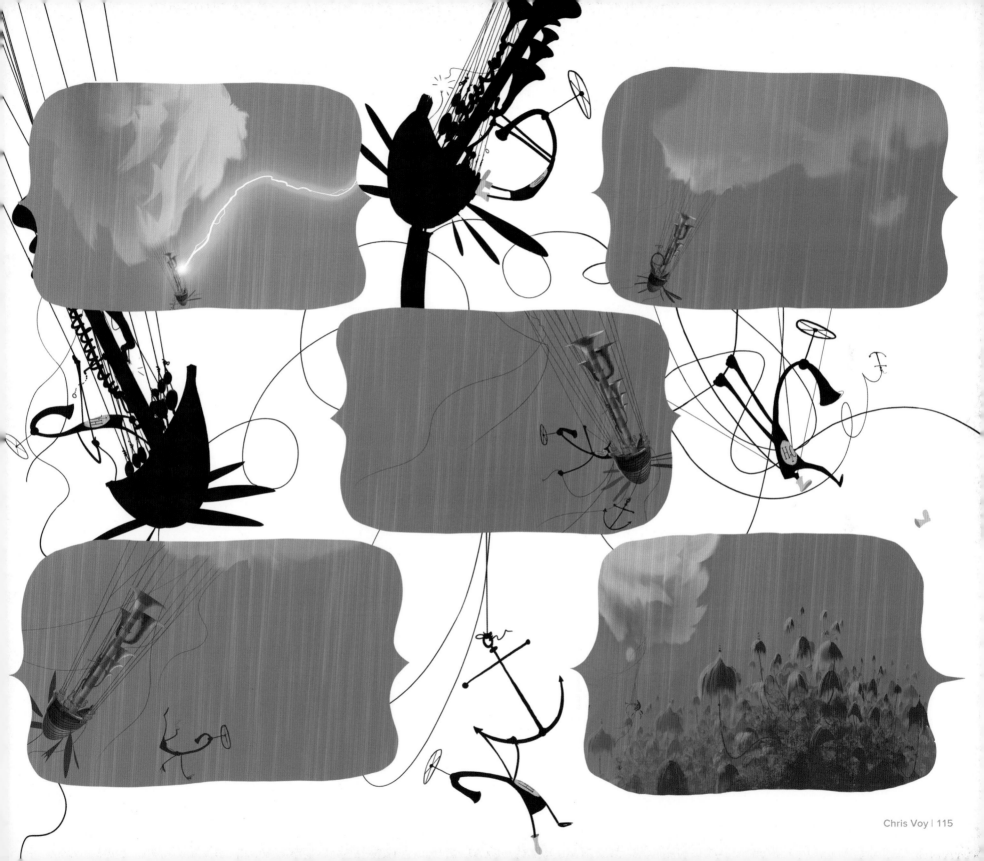

ABOUT THE ARTISTS

Amy Beth Christenson
In the time when the wind and thunder scarred the earth and galaxies from far, far away waged epic battle, one woman would rise—a mighty artist forged in the heart of the force. Throughout the galaxy she is known as LEGEND but for those who have met her, she is ABC.

Max Lim
My Korean name is Hyunwoo Lim. I was born in Korea. I got interested in art, particularly in becoming a concept artist. I thought that the profession seemed so fun and interesting because I'd be able to make every illusion and fantasy, and go between past and future. I have worked at Korean animation and game companies, and I eventually moved to San Francisco to attend the Academy of Art University where I majored in Animation Visual Development. Since graduation, I have worked as a concept designer at Lucasfilm Animation for Clone Wars, and now I am working as a senior concept artist at GREE, inc.

Jeff Sangalli
Jeff Sangalli was born and raised in the Bay Area. He studied Animation, Illustration, and Industrial Design at San José State University. He began his career at Pixar Feature Animation working on *Toy Story 2*. Jeff has enjoyed a diverse career working in film, games, print, and television at companies including Sony Computer Entertainment, LucasArts, National Geographic, Double Fine Productions, and Lucasfilm Animation. He has worked as both visual development artist and art director. Jeff has also continued to support the SJSU program as a guest lecturer and is dedicated to art and design education.

John-Paul Balmet
Born amidst the blazing oilfields of Bakersfield, California, J.P. caught a runaway tumbleweed North to the Bay Area. He found the way to San José, and there he studied under the relentless tutelage of the Shrunkenheadmen and their masters at San José State University. After learning their ways, he ventured forth into the world of concept art with employers such as Electronic Arts and Trion Worlds. A rolling stone gathers no moss, and J.P. eventually rolled into Lucasfilm Animation where he donned the mantle of concept designer on the animated television program *Star Wars: The Clone Wars*. In his spare time, J.P. sketches, writes stories, plays music, and tries to get out into nature whenever possible.

Will Nichols

In an age of legends and mystery, when man was yet new to earth, a gleaming kingdom laid shining in the West. The proudest city of this kingdom was Seattle, Washington. From whence was forged Will Nichols, born with pencil in hand. An artist warrior, a dreamer of worlds, with stories to tell and pictures to draw. Let him tell you of days of high adventure!

Nate Watson

Nate Watson entered the world of professional illustration after ten years of Service in the U.S. Air Force. He has since illustrated comic books featuring well-known properties including *Star Trek*, *Ghostbusters*, *Toy Story,* and *The Croods*. In 2010 he joined Lucasfilm Animation as a Visual Development artist on *Star Wars Detours*, and realized a lifelong dream of working in the field of animation. He is currently illustrating the digital-first comic series *The Incapeables* for Thrillbent, which by the time you read this, should be in its fifth month. In his oh-so-very-spare time, Nate enjoys cooking, archery, playing bass guitar and hanging out with his family. A native of Texas, Nate currently resides in Northern California with his wife Lynn and his four children.

Sean Pando

Sean has loved art as long as he can remember. This passion goes hand in hand with his love for animals. He frequently drew wildcats and planned to open a rehabilitation center for them. When Sean was 11 he painted a full-wall jungle mural in his bedroom, and almost managed to complete it without staining the carpet. He studied animation at Brigham Young University and was an art intern at Sony Online Entertainment illustrating trading cards. After graduation, Sean was thrilled to be hired at Lucasfilm Animation to work on *Star Wars Detours* as a concept artist. Sean lives in northern California and loves to surf on the weekends. Though he would still consider rescuing a wildcat, he will probably settle for getting a dog sometime in the near future.

Chris Voy

Deep in the wild bosom of Northern CA, a feral child emerged from the forest. He would not be schooled, nor was he very good at sports. Also, the girls were not too into him and so... he drew, damn it, he drew! And he painted and sometimes made things with Legos, then painted and drew some more, maybe rode his bike around for a bit, but always came back to paint. For many years it continued. He was not that great, but he kept trying because he was slightly better at painting than everything else. Now, thirty-something years later, he is pretty damn ok at it! He currently works at Lucasfilm Animation.

ACKNOWLEDGMENTS

This is dedicated to my amazing husband Dave Smith for acting as a single parent to Ellie while I finished this book. I can never thank you enough for being there for me 110% of the time, and I love you! And for my little Ellie Bean, the little bundle of awesome who showed up during the making of this book. I'd also like to thank my extended family and friends in Kansas, all of whom have supported and encouraged me my entire life, and to my friends and co-workers, especially the *Clone Wars* crew, *Punch Drunk* people, and *Battle Milk* folks. You are all great people and great artists, and I'm proud to be a part of it all.

—Amy Beth Christenson Smith

I would like to thank my wife Sehwon, daughter Dahin, and God, the Jesus Christ, for everything, my fellow *Punch Drunk* crew, my *Clone Wars* animation concept team for giving passion, my Korean friends, GMS group for giving motivation and my Academy of Art University teachers Chuck Pyle and Terryl Whitlatch.

—Max Lim (Hyunwoo Lim)

This is dedicated to an amazing mentor, artist, and father, Richard A. Sangalli. I'd like to thank Alice Carter and Courtney Granner for their continued guidance and support throughout my career. I feel fortunate to have had the chance to work with the talented *Punch Drunk* crew. Lastly, thank you to my wife, Kim, and son, Dominic for their patience and love.

—Jeff Sangalli

I would like to thank: My lovely wife and editor Kristel, my friends and family, my fellow *Punch Drunk* crew, the *Battle Milk* guys, especially Kilian, Pat, and Jackson, Scott Robertson and Design Studio Press for taking a chance, Tinti, Wilfred, Bunny Carter, Dave Chai, my Clone Wars design compadres, James Gurney, Dermot Power, Chee Fong, Jens Holdener, Jesse Lee, Konstantin Abadjiev, the old master painters and illustrators I admire and emulate, Katsuhiro Otomo, the Shrunkenheadmen and the Animation/Illustration SJSU program, and of course, God for peace, patience and inspiration.

—John-Paul Balmet

There are so many people to thank for getting me this far. First and foremost, my family for always nurturing and believing in my dream of becoming an artist. To all my friends in Washington and Lucasfilm Animation, especially Clone Wars team, *Punch Drunk Moustache*, and *Battle Milk*, thanks for all the support and encouragement. I am blessed to know such amazing people and I am very proud and humbled to be a part of this collection of incredible talent.

—Will Nichols

The Creator, for sharing His talent with me. My wife Lynn for years of support, encouragement, honesty and tolerance—and my kiddos: Chance, Aysia, Ethan, Jordan, Bethany Joy and Joseph for sharing daddy with this very time-consuming profession. Love you all!

And, in no particular order: Brendan Hay, Steve Wyatt, Mom C., Mom K., Dad, *Punch Drunk* crew, the *Detours* team, Vi and J.B. (Miss you, dude), Tom Gregor, Quincy Stamper and Bill at Blue Sky photography, Mark Waid, Mark Dobrin, Mark Cox, the *Battle Milk* crew (at least Killian

and Pat), and Ryan Sook. All of you, in some way or another, helped me get XB3 done!
—**Nate Watson**

The Lord, for the all the guidance and blessings in my life. My incredible family, my mom and dad for being so supportive of my art and everything else, and my three amazing siblings, Derek, Alina and Brian, who are my greatest friends. My 6th grade art teacher, Karri Clark. Also Oscar Galvan, Robert Barrett, Ryan Woodward, Brent Adams, Kelly Loosli, Derek Herring, David Mc-Clellan, and everyone else who has supported me. All my *Detours* coworkers that have had the patience to help me and have taught me loads! Especially Micah Sibert, and Martin Kau. Jeff Sangalli for being the best mentor I could hope to work with. And finally the *Punch Drunk* artists who were kind enough to let me be a part of this amazing project!
—**Sean Pando**

First, to my amazing wife, Brandi: after long workdays you've been Supermom to Jules and Ali while I worked into the wee hours-even after

I kept saying I was "almost done." Thank you for being so patient, supportive and understanding through this. I love you. Thank you to my parents for always telling me how much they loved my drawings and paintings and encouraging me when I had a long way to go. Also, thanks for ordering a bunch of copies of this book before most of us started working on it! Thanks to all my sisters and their families, the Orsats and the rest of the *PDM* crew. I love all you guys!
—**Chris Voy**

AFTERWORD

While I was a wide-eyed art student at San José State University, I was given an invaluable chunk of advice from one of the big moustached alum. He told me and some of my peach-fuzzed upper lippers that some of the best times he had in school and biggest lessons he learned weren't from a class, or an instructor, or an art book, but from doing personal projects with fellow students. I, along with some of my classmates, took his advice and did just that. And... he was right! There was no pressure to get a good grade or impress an instructor, just to have fun sharing our passion for what we all came to school to do—tell compelling stories through provocative imagery, learn, and have fun. The champ with the impressive stash, worn leather gloves, endless words of wisdom and encouragement was none other than *Punch Drunk Moustache* boxer extraordinaire Jeff Sangalli!

This book is a perfect example of the passion project work Jeff was telling us about. Eight artists doing work they want to do, not worrying about what test audiences might think, if they're going to get a good grade or not, or how many tickets it will sell. The artwork represented in this book truly looks as if the artists that created it had fun doing so.

If you've purchased this book, then chances are you're an artist of some form or another. At this point you've already ingested the book's awe-inspiring visual content. Which means you're not even reading this afterword because after taking in the power that is *Punch Drunk Moustache*, you picked up a pencil, a paintbrush, or more likely a stylus (kids these days), and have been pumping out some inspirational work of your own. Why did I bother even writing this? Damn you *Punch Drunk Moustache*! Damn you! Forget this afterword nonsense... I'm going to go draw!

—Colin Fix

Thank you for purchasing Punch Drunk Moustache.
For more information about the artists,
visit **punchdrunkmoustache.blogspot.com**